Silver Linings

Meditations on Finding Joy and Beauty in Unexpected Places

Mina Parker

PHOTOGRAPHS BY DANIEL TALBOTT

Silver Linings

Meditations on Finding Joy and Beauty in Unexpected Places

Conari Press

First published in 2008 by Conari Press,
an imprint of Red Wheel/Weiser, LLC
With offices at:
500 Third Street, Suite 230
San Francisco, CA 94107
www.redwheelweiser.com

ISBN-13: 978-1-57324-361-2
Library of Congress Cataloging-in-Publication Data
Parker, Mina.
Silver linings: meditations on finding joy and beauty in unexpected
places/Mina Parker; photos by Daniel Talbott.
    p. cm.
  ISBN 978-1-57324-361-2 (alk. paper)
1. Joy. 2. Aesthetics. I. Talbott, Daniel. II. Title.
  BJ1481.P37 2008
  158.1'28–dc22
2008009108

Cover and text design by Maija Tollefson
Typeset in Joanna
Cover photograph © Daniel Talbott

printed in Hong Kong
SS
10 9 8 7 6 5 4 3 2 1

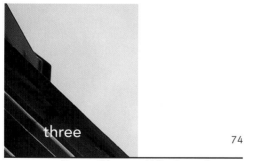
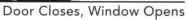

Introduction

Every cloud has a silver lining.

— PROVERB

My two-year-old son recently learned the game "I Spy," and now a couple of times a day he'll say in a sing-song voice:

"I spy with my little eye something that is . . . blue."

And then we look around trying to find the blue things, the red things, the green things, and so on. One day we were in a place without much color at all, and I said, "I spy with my little eye something that is . . . gray!" He wasn't quite clear on the color gray, so he pointed to a pole on the subway. "Sure," I said, "that's sort of gray. Actually it's silver. That's shiny gray."

The description made me smile. Usually gray is a downer—dreary, drab, or gloomy. Dismal overcast skies, or dreaded gray hair, or an ashen face when you hear terrible news. But often, all it takes to see the good in the darkest gray moment is to shed a little light on it. Shine up that old gray and you get silver, and suddenly the whole world looks brighter.

It's no secret that looking on the bright side makes for a better life. Optimists live longer, are healthier, and have fewer wrinkles than the rest of us. Okay, I made that last one up, but

7

even if they have the same number of wrinkles—or more—the lines somehow make them look wiser, not older. To top that off, I just read one of those odd statistics that says that people who are happy earn on average three-quarters of a million dollars more in their lifetimes than people who aren't happy. Well, this book isn't about earning money, but that's a nice, if true, factoid.

It doesn't take much to shine up your old outlook or try on a new one. I come from a long line of pessimistic optimists. You know the type—people who imagine the worst so they can be pleasantly surprised now and then. One of my grandfather's favorite sayings was "Into each life a little rain must fall." I must have heard it a thousand times before I was ten, and I always understood it the same way: when it rains on your parade you'll be better off if you remember there's bound to be disappointment and heartache in life, and if you mentally prep for the worst, you'll be able to get over it quickly and easily.

More recently I've started to rethink the meaning of this saying. Maybe you don't have to spend your days and nights constructing mental rain shelters in preparation for the great flood that may or may not ever come. Maybe, if you can see the positive even in the worst situations, that outlook can be its own rainy-day relief.

Only in the past few years have I started to see the value of being an unabashed optimist. I can't always muster it, and sometimes I'll admit it takes me quite a while to see the good in certain situations, but I've learned that the worst I get from trying is a giggle or two at my own expense.

This is a book to lighten the darker moments and revel in the brighter ones. I've collected quotes and stories to help me on my way; I hope they help you to reflect on your outlook, notice the beauty in even the hardest situations, make the most of unexpected events, and celebrate the beauty of coming through hardship and pain to the other side.

In addition to the words, I've included photos that I hope will inspire and comfort you. Daniel Talbott set out on a daily basis to take these photos, noticing the beauty all around us all the time: the momentary reflections in shop windows, quiet moments, and most important, flowers. Flowers bursting out in unlikely cityscapes, thriving in all seasons and all places. Lots and lots and lots of flowers, because they are the best symbols of silver linings: the products of bright sunny days and heavy dark rain clouds. I hope you'll find the beauty of these images a balm for the tough times, and the meditations and stories a refreshing take on finding and keeping a positive outlook through all kinds of weather. You'll be spotting the silver linings all around you in no time.

One
What You See Is What You Get

What You See Is What You Get

"What you see is what you get." A while ago I thought of this saying as negative. No frills, no surprises, no hidden value. As I get older, though, I appreciate simplicity more and more. It used to be, in relationships, work projects, and even leisure time, I thought a little complication or ambiguity added spice. But really, the simplest things are the most mysterious, engaging, and profound. People who are straightforward and don't pretend to be anything more or less than they are are the most fascinating to be around. Getting what you see and seeing what you get is a blessing.

Beyond that, the saying alludes to the untapped power of your individual outlook. People who develop a gift for looking on the bright side get more out of life. Developing the habit of seeing the good things around you goes a long way toward improving your day-to-day existence. Remembering to share your gratitude helps, too.

Silver Medal

Too many people miss the silver lining because they're
expecting gold.

—MAURICE SETTER

Sometimes I can't see clearly. Without my glasses everything's
fuzzy—trees are green blobs, faces are blank at any distance
beyond 4 feet, and, worst of all, I can't find my glasses
anywhere. This problem with my eyes is a metaphor, too.
Sometimes I can't see the world clearly. My mental outlook
clouds my sensory and intellectual experiences, and I decide
what I'm seeing before I even see it.

Give yourself a silver medal as a reminder that there are more important things in life than the pursuit of perfection.

Everything has a silver lining, a good side, a positive spin.
A glass with even a drop in it is on the way to full, and if it's
totally empty, it's full of potential. It's not always easy to see
the silver lining in a dark cloud, and sometimes it's hard to
believe in it when we do see it. The worst of all is to miss it
completely because of our own fuzziness (or fussiness) as we
wait for a perfection that can never be realized.

If you're planning some absolute future happiness that
requires a huge dollar amount, an ideal partner, and an easy
daily existence, think again. Set a goal that is unattainable, and
you are sure to come up short. Here's an idea: Challenge
yourself to reach concrete goals that are farther away and
more difficult than any you've imagined before. Know you
can do it, work toward it with an open heart, and you can't
go wrong. Even if you don't meet your original goal, I guar-
antee you will find a more meaningful path along the way.

Guitar Practice

Every kind of music is good, except the boring kind.
— GIOACCHINO ROSSINI

What rewards will you earn through your everyday activities, even the ones that aren't so much fun?

My parents gave me some wonderful gifts as a child—things that took practice and patience and you could never really get too good at to get bored. One of my favorites of these was an acoustic guitar. I couldn't wait to get started playing. I had a book of chords, but it seemed too hard, so I gave up trying to figure it out pretty quickly. I really couldn't play at all. I just plucked and strummed the open strings of the guitar over and over again, spending hours making up new plucking combinations and seeing how fast I could do them and which ones went together. If anyone had been listening, I don't think they would've thought much of the music I was making. I eventually got quite frustrated myself, and set it aside.

It was only later when a teacher at school helped me learn some basic chords and songs that I realized the upside of my earlier experience. Unlike most beginner players, I could figure out complicated fingerings and picking patterns quickly, because I had practiced myself to the brink of exhaustion without ever getting the payoff of making real music.

I wonder if some of the mundane tasks I do every day are building skills that will pay dividends later. Even if it's just the daily tasks of maintaining my health—brushing teeth, exercising, eating well—those should certainly pay off later.

Cherry Blossoms

Break open a cherry tree and there are no flowers, but the
spring breeze brings forth myriad blossoms.

— IKKYU SOJUN

My friend Julie is obsessed with cherry blossoms, particularly
with the annual springtime festival celebrating them at our
local botanical gardens. She spends the weeks and days leading
up to the festival checking the "blossom watch" on the garden's
Website, a map of the varietals and their estimated peak days.
She can distinguish the scent and color differences between
trees and has her favorites. If you've never stood in the middle
of a group of cherry trees in full blossom, you might think
she's a bit bonkers—or eccentric at the very least. If you've
been lucky enough to get up close, to feel the petals brush your
nose, to immerse yourself in that light perfume, you know.

> *Find, pick, smell,*
> *taste something at*
> *its peak—a fruit,*
> *a flower, a bottle*
> *of wine.*

But they don't last. That's why you really need the blossom
watch. So you can catch the peak moment—because after that
a few big gusts of wind create a spring blizzard of petals, and
then the cherry trees look like all the rest. I've always thought
of that as sad—why do they have to pass so quickly? What's
the point of all that effort—millions of petals gone within a
day or two? Julie isn't fazed in the least. She revels in the tem-
porary beauty—a great reminder to be present where you are,
to enjoy the vista right in front of you, and to appreciate that
every single thing has its perfect time and place.

The Upside-Down Side

Humor is merely tragedy standing on its head with its pants torn.

—Irvin S. Cobb

Sometimes the best way to find the upside of a problem or situation is to find a way to turn it upside down.

One of the great gifts I can thank my husband for is something he's shown me through action time and again. When he's in a tough situation at work, or with a friend, or in any other aspect of his life, he has an almost magical ability to flip it and turn it around for the better. It's almost counterintuitive, and that, coupled with his healthy sense of humor, may be the secret of why it works.

If you've lost something—stop looking for it. Do something else totally unrelated and your subconscious will lead you right to what you were looking for.

If someone is rude to you—apologize to them. It will certainly take them by surprise, and it may remind them of their own forgotten manners.

If you want to kick a bad habit, like complaining, try a full day of super-loud complaining at absolutely everything. Go ahead, get dramatic, be loud and silly and over the top. Have your fill of it, and then let it go.

Recycling

Every silver lining has a cloud. All the glasses that seemed
half-full twelve months ago look half-empty now.
— CHARLES CRANE

Welcome to the dumps. You've been here before; you know
all the familiar sights. There's a burbling brook of guilt and
grief running through a valley of sleepless nights. The glasses
are bone dry, and the rose-colored specs are cracked. From
where you're standing, it doesn't look like things are going to
get any better.

When I find myself in this terrain, I know I'm in trouble.
Sometimes I get sick and have to lie in bed for a week.
Sometimes I'm a pill to the people I love. Sometimes it's less
obvious, but I can still feel it—a nagging pessimism I just
can't shake. The dumps are an okay place to visit, but I really
don't want to live there.

In San Francisco, there is a garbage dump that's been
repurposed as a place where artists and schoolchildren come
to find recycled material to make their art. Maybe I can apply
this idea to my mental dump—there must be something in
there worth taking out, taking apart, and refashioning into
something beautiful or meaningful.

*Start a recycling program
in your mind. Depression
into recuperation. Anger
into reflection. Difficulty
into exciting challenge.*

Semiprecious

It is perhaps a more fortunate destiny to have a taste for collecting shells than to be born a millionaire.

—Robert Louis Stevenson

Make a tally of your true net worth—including the people and things you love.

The word *semiprecious* refers to stones that are less commercially valuable than rubies and diamonds but cost more than gravel. Sometimes a lot more. It seems a bit arbitrary—which shiny stone is better, after all? I love mother of pearl, and turquoise, and I like wearing silver more than gold most of the time. In thinking about silver linings, the word semiprecious popped into my head. And I think it's time to throw it away.

I'm sick of semiprecious. If we value everything solely based upon the price it can fetch, what do we have? I've watched friends' artistic talents shrivel in the face of their dread at not being marketable. Some other task, like writing advertising copy, seemed more reliable, so they sidelined their art in favor of more solid commercial prospects. Phooey.

The true value of things grows through the acts of love we contribute to them. Sometimes we think the only way we'll be happy or satisfied is to succeed in the eyes of others or to meet some predetermined standard of stability or riches. Really, we should count ourselves lucky for all the plentiful sources of wealth around us. Like shell collecting, making conversation, gardening, refining a skill, or sitting down with a good book.

New Neighborhood

Nothing in life is to be feared. It is only to be understood.

— M A R I E C U R I E

Last year my husband and I found that our apartment was too small for our growing family, and we made the move to a bigger place. We moved into a bigger space we could afford—a beautiful, spacious place in a neighborhood we'd never visited before. We were pretty spooked by a fatal stabbing on the front stoop ("Don't worry," the landlord reassured us, "they were friends"). We considered leaving, but we loved the apartment, and our immediate neighbors were incredibly sweet and kind.

So we decided to work on noticing the things we loved about our new digs. The architecture of the apartment itself, how quiet it was, the smells of elaborate Sunday dinners cooking throughout the building. Instead of looking at some of the downers of the place and the locale and regretting our decision, we resolved to do one thing each week to spruce it up and make it an oasis for our family.

It worked. What felt foreign and scary now feels like home, and the whole experience has broadened our perspective and renewed our faith in a proactive, positive approach.

Home is where your heart is, and comfort is what you make it.

Head in the Clouds

The difference between visionaries and dreamers is that visionaries make the dreams come true.

— WALTER R. MUELLER

In my family we have a pet theory about people falling roughly into two camps—the Clouds and the Bricks. Clouds are the dreamers, the ones who free-associate and have wild imaginations. The Bricks are the stable ones—pragmatic, focused, taking charge, and getting stuff done. We found at some point that these clichés weren't quite descriptive enough. So then some more categories were invented:

"Oh, she's a Cloud masquerading as a Brick." Meaning she has a talent for getting things done and wants to be taken seriously, but underneath it all she's a bit of an airhead who gets lost in thought and forgets to bring home dinner.

Or, "He's a Brick who wishes he was a Cloud." Meaning he wants to be carefree and flighty and blow off his responsibilities, but at his core he cares too much about security and solidity.

All of this describing and revising made for fun at family get-togethers, and I started to realize that any stereotype contains multitudes of possibilities within it. You may think you have someone pinned—your boss, your mother, your best friend. But their silver lining might surprise you. A tough guy with a soft spot for abandoned animals. A miser who contributes regularly and anonymously to her favorite charity. You never know.

Are you a Cloud? A Brick? Or floating somewhere in between?

Laugh Your Troubles Away

And if I laugh at any mortal thing,
'Tis that I may not weep.

— Lord Byron

Finding what's funny in a tough situation is the fastest road to recovery.

Laughing and crying in the same breath—ever done it? You're so overwhelmed, miserable, and tired that you can't help but laugh when one more thing comes your way? Laughing is probably the best tool we have to see the good in things.

On the day I was born, my father rushed to the hospital, and when he got there realized he'd forgotten to let the dog out. He called a neighbor kid who went to the house and found that the dog was already out in the yard, so the kid got confused and put the dog in. When my father got home early the next morning, he found the dog sitting in the middle of a completely destroyed house. Every book was off the shelf and well chewed. The sofa pillows were emptied of stuffing, the shoes scattered. My father lost it—the stress and excitement of a new baby mixed with the lack of sleep and facing an utter disaster just did him in.

He couldn't stop giggling. The dog padded around after him as he cleaned up the house. He would squelch the laughter for a while and then it would come back stronger than ever. He said he felt so silly, but he really just had to laugh it out. And then he got to tell the whole story to friends and family (with photographic evidence, of course) and that spread the laughter around in the best way. It makes sense to me, and it sure kept him from crying!

Either/Or, Both/And

The glass is either half-full, or half-empty, or both.

— MY MOTHER-IN-LAW

Ever spent any time with one of those people for whom there is no middle ground? A friend who threatens to break off a close relationship at a slight disagreement? Or a coworker who refuses to negotiate a different plan, even if the first one isn't getting results? Some people can see the glass only as half-full or half-empty, so they go through life swinging back and forth between the extremes of good and bad, thrilled and miserable, winning and losing.

Don't miss seeing the cloud for the lining, or the lining for the cloud.

People with a gift for seeing silver linings know there is hope somewhere between the extremes. Don't get me wrong, there are times that a radical stance is the only way to go, and I'm not championing a general wishy-washy approach to life. Unlike the glass, which is supposedly either half-full or half-empty, the cloud and its silver lining are an integral whole. One could not exist without the other, and together they provide a fuller understanding of the ups as well as the downs.

I'm going to practice seeing both sides of every situation and changing my either/or attitude into a both/and one. Even if things around me don't improve right away, I'm sure my feelings about my circumstances will be a lot more positive, and that in itself will make my life better.

The Light Behind

And as we let our own light shine, we unconsciously give other people permission to do the same.

—NELSON MANDELA

If something doesn't look right one way or the other, try shining a light from all sides and see what happens.

When we used to take family pictures as a kid I remember my dad always standing us in the spot with the most sunshine, facing right into the bright light. He thought that made for the best photos. Needless to say, most every picture I have of my family has us all squinting into the lens, trying our best keep our eyelids open in the glare.

When I started taking my own pictures I decided to try the opposite approach, with the sun behind whoever I was photographing. Well, the subjects were a lot more comfortable, but the pictures were miserable—everyone had bright halos of hair and dark, featureless faces.

Then I read a photo tip that said to keep that same position but turn on the flash. This melded both theories and proved to be by far the best. Now I happily flash away on bright sunny days at the beach, and I get people with eyes, noses, and that lovely backlight. Looking at the photos, you can almost feel the warm sun on your back.

Doors, Windows, and Seeing More Clearly

All other things being equal, the simplest explanation is the best.

— WILLIAM OF OCKHAM

"You make a better door than window!" I remember another kid screaming that at me from the back of a room of children watching a movie on a special day at school. I was totally stumped. I'd never heard the saying and I couldn't parse it. My best friend yanked me down by my shirtsleeve and whispered, "It means sit down." That did nothing to help my understanding, but it did stop the kid who was shouting at me, and that was a relief.

I thought about that saying for a long time, sure there was some complicated meaning to it. Am I a door to another world? Or do kids think that windows are better because they let in the sunshine? "Just means they can't see through you, honey," my grandma finally explained.

Aha!—the light bulb went off, and it was the first of many concrete reminders I've gotten to remember that sometimes the simplest approach or answer leads to the greatest understanding.

If you're having trouble figuring out a problem, try the most literal, simple answer you can think of.

31

The Perfect Whole

When you realize how perfect everything is you will tilt your
head back and laugh at the sky.

— BUDDHA

*Try the practice of moving
beyond judgment and feel-
ing that everything that
happens is meant to be.*

Nothing in this world is wrong or bad. Everything happens
for a reason. Everything is meant to be. This is the basic wisdom behind so many mystical and spiritual traditions, but it's
probably the most difficult to understand. How can the death
of a child be okay? How can injustice and poverty be a part
of any grand scheme? I don't know—I'm not at the laughing-
up-at-the-sky moment by any far stretch. It's a long road to
that kind of enlightenment.

I do know that the few moments of perfection I've
glimpsed somehow go beyond, or incorporate, all that is
"good" or "bad" in the world. In a moment of intense joy or
pain, or even a moment of eminent danger, like the seconds
before a car crash, people report feeling a sense of calm and
unity that transcends judgment. Even outside of those
moments of intensity, we can find ways to extend the limits
of what we think of as good and bad and to give over to a
universal power that is both part of us and beyond us.

Rediscovery

Everything of importance has already been seen by
somebody who didn't notice it.

— ALFRED NORTH WHITEHEAD

*Take a day to rediscover
your noticing skills—
write down what you
see, think, and feel
without judgment.*

I've read that any great discovery—whether in science, art,
literature, or philosophy—is not really a new discovery. It is
a rearranged picture puzzle of readily available information.
So genius isn't as much about sitting around dreaming up
new things as it is about dreaming up new ways for old
things to fit together.

The building blocks for every discovery that will ever be
made are already here—all around us, all the time. It only
takes open eyes and an open heart. I had a teacher once who
discouraged the phrase *Pay attention* and preferred the word
Notice. A subtle difference, sure, but an important one. When
you have to pay attention, you put pressure on yourself. You
demand that your brain do as it is told, and in the process the
filter that tells you what you should or should not be paying
attention to confines you. When you let yourself *notice* what
you are seeing without judging whether or not it is worthy
of your attention, you find a wealth of new information at
your fingertips and are free to start to put the pieces together
in a whole new way.

Eyes Wide Open

One of the most wonderful things in nature is a glance
of the eye; it transcends speech; it is the bodily symbol
of identity.

—RALPH WALDO EMERSON

One day I was late. Later than late. One of those days you leave the house ten minutes later than you would've liked, then watch the train or bus pull away before you can catch up to it. Throw in a couple more delays and travel snafus and a nice snarly traffic jam—that was the day I was having. Forty-five minutes after the start of my meeting, I was pacing at the end of a dark and smelly subway station, with no train in sight and the platform getting more and more crowded with people in a similar state of stress.

I tried to remind myself that it was out of my hands, knowing my anxiety would only make things worse. Trying to jostle my mind out of its cycle of blame, worry, and frustration, I started looking around.

A warning sign about rodenticide. Yuck. Gum stuck to the column in front of me at eye level. Gross. Then something caught my eye. A leak from the ceiling was spreading rusty water down the wall. Where the water ran onto a poster, the layers of paper had started to peel away, revealing a mosaic of colors of all the other posters underneath. Ads for beer and singles Websites and health care for underprivileged kids. I imagined it would make a beautiful abstract photo in someone's house. Lost in those thoughts, I forgot for a moment how late I was, and the train rolled in before I knew it.

Savor the gift of really looking around, especially in anxious or frustrating times.

35

Catch a Rainbow

The true harvest of my life is intangible—a little star dust
caught, a portion of the rainbow I have clutched.

—HENRY DAVID THOREAU

In the late 1660s Sir Isaac Newton started doing experiments
with prisms and figured out that white light contains all the
colors in the spectrum. Before that, the pervading theory was
that colors were a mixture of light and dark, each falling
somewhere between bright red and pitch black. Prisms, it
was thought, were making the colors, not refracting them. I
still remember being skeptical when I learned as a kid that all
the colors of the rainbow were a part of white light. It didn't
make any sense—how come you couldn't see them?

Hang a prism in your window, and you might see a rainbow on a cloudy day.

What a discovery. Every bit of light in the world has a
rainbow hidden in it. If it didn't, we wouldn't be able to see
color as we know it. That secret color is an inspiration to me.
If something seems boring, bland, or washed out, I only have
to remember the rainbows inside. If a problem seems impos-
sible to solve, or the solutions look just as grim, I try to find
the hidden colors. They are there—and I don't even need a
prism to look at them; my own mind, just as it is, is the perfect tool. After all, as Newton found out, a prism doesn't *make*
colors; it doesn't have to *do* anything—just let the light filter
through and *voilà*.

Turn, Turn, Turn

Everything in life that we really accept undergoes a change. So suffering must become love. That is the mystery.

—KATHERINE MANSFIELD

Trust that the cycle of life will bring understanding, will help us transform pain into love through our acceptance.

Life comes in cycles. Births and deaths, beginnings and endings. This can be a source of apprehension or one of comfort, depending on how you look at it. I have read countless stories of tragedies or struggles that test the strength and bonds of friendship and family. Those who are able to accept their circumstances and work through them together come through them stronger and better off.

I just read about a woman who nursed her husband back to health over the course of two years after a devastating car crash. She related that people often ask her, "How did you do it?" Her answer was that she never asked herself how they were going to do it, or how he was going to heal, they just did it.

Not asking how, just doing it. After the initial shock of a tragedy or loss there is an eventual understanding and acceptance that allows for action to take over—the just doing it. Suffering leads to understanding, understanding brings knowledge, and knowledge breeds love. As you face a problem and invest in a solution and work on it, the love grows all around you. Even on the hardest emotional ground, new understanding, love, and deeper bonds can sprout and grow.

It's All Relative

One man's poison ivy is another man's spinach.

— George Ade

I remember going off to college and playing one of those getting-to-know-each-other games with a small group of people. Somehow the game transformed into an airing of family histories, and there were some interesting ones: a vaudevillian grandmother, an uncle busted for smuggling drugs in his underpants, a maiden aunt who ate nothing but cold cereal for the last five years of her life.

And then there was Danielle. She started to talk about her family and her childhood, and we all listened with our mouths practically hanging open. Her history was like a Russian novel crossed with a Greek myth and set in the deep, gothic South. She told it all pretty matter-of-factly, with patches of humor and self-deprecating wit. When she had finished we all felt a little silly for thinking our families were crazy, considering how nuts her stories were. She put it all in perspective, however, by saying, "I truly believe that no one has a normal family. Everyone has to survive their own version of family insanity, and from the inside they can't be compared."

If someone who'd been through that much could have that perspective, I thought, it might be an important lesson for dealing with others.

Just because you are having a harder or easier time than someone else doesn't mean comparisons would be helpful.

The Shining Darkness

I shut my eyes in order to see.

— PAUL GAUGUIN

As a kid I went on a school trip to Yosemite, and on one moonless night we were led on a mile-long walk. Each kid was sent off three minutes or so ahead of the next one, so the only sounds you heard were of the wind in the leaves, and the stars shed the only light on the path. Up until that point in my life I had never been so alone in such darkness before, and the feeling shot straight through my gut.

Deprived of sight, all my other senses woke up and started working overtime. I could smell the campfire I'd just walked away from more clearly than when I'd been standing next to it. I could hear a waterfall and made out the sound of bat wings scooping up insects in the trees. I started to walk more confidently, sensing the path even though I couldn't see my own feet in the blackness.

It's true that our eyes play tricks on us. Our brain is only doing its job when it shortcuts real sensation by guessing what's going on. We don't have to smell a fire if we see it next to us, so we cut out that sensory middleman. Close your eyes, and new vistas open as new sensation and information floods in.

Take a walk in the dark—even through your own home— and see things in a new light.

41

Deep Water

Man cannot discover new oceans unless he has the courage
to lose sight of the shore.

— ANDRE GIDE

*When's the last time
you left the shore of
your comfort level?*

I don't actually remember my first experience with deep
water. My mom tells this story. She had taken me to a swimming beach at a lake near our house. I was about two. I
caught sight of a lot of bigger kids laughing, squealing, and
jumping off a pontoon about 50 feet from shore. I guess it
looked like fun to me, or at least that's what my mom says. I
took off at a full tilt. I was up to my eyebrows by the time she
caught me. And when she scooped me up, I arched my back
and tried to get free. I was headed for that pontoon and all
that fun, come heck or high water.

My mom had worked hard to get over her own fear of
deep water. She tells the story of her mother standing on the
shore, sucking in breath through her teeth, muttering, "Don't
let her drown," as my grandfather tried to teach her to swim.
The fear of deep water, or lack of it, seems to be about what
each of us were seeing. As a two year old I saw only fun and
adventure, while my grandmother had her eyes peeled for
possible disaster. Neither my mom nor I are going to discover
any new oceans (at least I don't think we are) but both of us
have found our own ways to lose sight of the shore in search
of new adventures.

Two

Beauty Grows on Hard Ground

Beauty Grows on Hard Ground

I was at a kid's soccer game a while ago, and when the team started to make a few mistakes, missing easy shots, the coach shouted out, "Aware-ify!" It seemed to work for the players, it perked up the fans, and playing improved right away. Now when things start to look bland or downright dreadful, I give myself a mental shout to aware-ify, to take in the world around me, hear the background noise, to stop and smell the flowers. I notice all sorts of things—sweet conversations overheard on the street, an intricate design over a doorway, even little sparkles in some concrete down the street. It's like finding bite-sized bits of beauty all over, and it sustains and refreshes my outlook.

Sometimes I find the most rewarding tidbits in the least likely places: bright orange poppies thriving on a highway divider, a tree growing in the tiny space between two buildings, or a splash of color courtesy of a graffiti artist. The beauty that stands out in contrast to bleak surroundings sneaks up on us to lavish its rewards. Playing this kind of hide and seek will always lead you to a brighter, happier state of being.

Trash and Treasure

Let no one who loves be unhappy. . . . Even love
unreturned has its rainbow.

— J. M. BARRIE

*Look for treasure
all around.*

The lopped off head of a sunflower, dropped on someone's
front step. I can't help it, I started to imagine stories. A
woman digs for her keys while trying to juggle five bags of
groceries for dinner with the in-laws. "Damn it, I knew these
flowers didn't look fresh at the market. There they go, just
falling apart."

Or worse, "No, no, no, flowers aren't going to get you
out of this one, you jerk. You can keep them!"

Or maybe the story has a sweet ending. A boy and a girl,
hand in hand down the street. She glances at it lying on the
stoop. They walk by. Five steps later he turns, runs back,
retrieves it for her. She blushes.

Things fall apart. Plans, projects, relationships. It may
seem that when something falls apart or breaks, it's useless.
Not so. The end of a relationship means two people wiser and
more seasoned. Dinner not coming together just so means it's
time to trust your improvisational skills, and the results will
be better than you could have ever planned for (or you'll have
a good excuse to try that new restaurant down the block).
When it comes to throwing something out and moving on,
remember the packrat's mantra: "One person's trash is another
person's treasure."

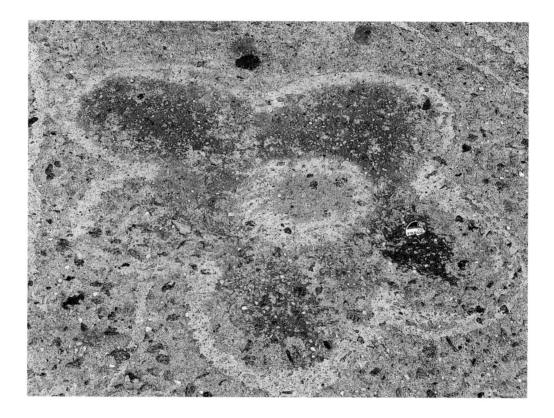

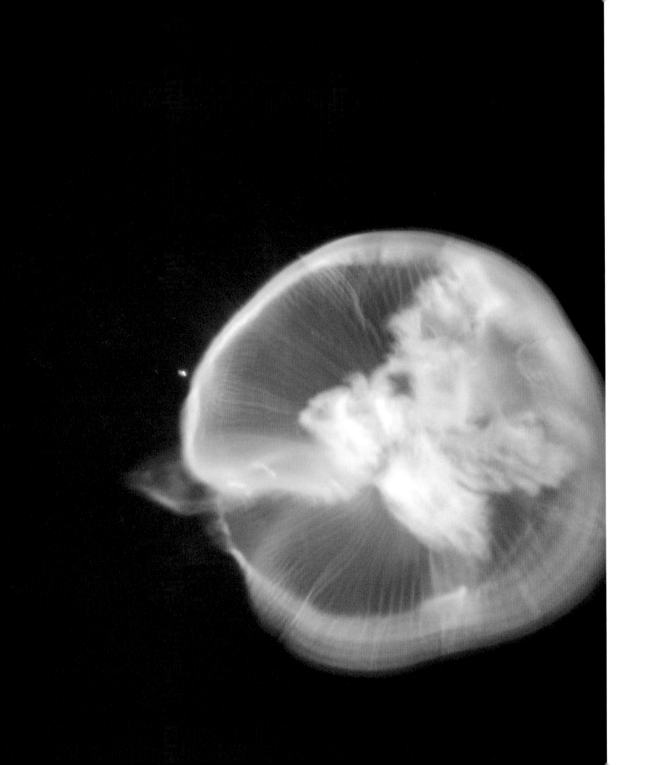

Jellyfish Lining

The water in a vessel is sparkling; the water in the sea is dark. The small truth has words which are clear; the great truth has great silence.

— RABINDRANATH TAGORE

Last year I went with my family to a jellyfish exhibit at the Monterey Bay Aquarium. It was dimly lit, and the jellyfish glowed, suspended in the darkness.

Sometimes it takes looking at something from a safe distance to see the beauty in it.

My only previous experience with jellies had been on a Delaware beach where I was too afraid to swim because of the piles of gooey dead jellyfish washed on shore. That and watching a screaming kid run out of the water with big red welts (don't ask me what his parents were thinking). I was happy to be on the other side of the glass, away from those filmy tentacles filled with poison. But at the exhibit I saw that even jellyfish have a silver lining! The edges of their bodies glow. They're gorgeous. I stayed for nearly an hour, totally lost in that world.

Green Power

He is happiest who hath power to gather wisdom
from a flower.

— MARY HOWITT

When we feel alone,
exhausted, or down-
trodden, we can
remember that the
flowers are finding a
way, and so can we.

I remember the relief and excitement that came with the end
of a long winter when I was a kid—the days getting brighter
and longer, the snow starting to melt, the birds coming back.
One April day I saw little purple flowers coming up through
the inch or so of snow left on the ground in our yard—cro-
cuses. It seemed too good to be true that a flower could burst
out of patches of snow and ice.

Certain flowers and plants find a way to live and thrive in
the most extreme places and climates. In deserts, on mountain peaks, in caves, even in dim city apartments. One of my
favorite recent examples of this is that humans have planted
more than 1 billion trees in the past year, more than half of
them in sub-Saharan Africa in and around the expanding
deserts there. The trees take root and thrive in the harsh conditions, and in the process they hold water in the soil and
prevent erosion and dune migration. People can farm and
graze their animals, and therefore survive.

Flowers and plants sprouting and thriving in unlikely
places seems like a perfect image to remind us that even in
difficult conditions we can fulfill our destiny and make our
lives beautiful.

Vandal Trees

Fortunate are the people whose roots are deep.

— AGNES MAYER

I read somewhere once that trees are by far the strongest living things on the planet in terms of the pounds of force they can exert per square inch. It makes sense—even a full-grown elephant might have trouble forcing a pliable root through a solid concrete block, something trees accomplish everywhere all the time. Property owners cringe, cement mixers celebrate, and you've got to admire that kind of power coming from something that doesn't sport so much as a bicep.

In almost any situation, there's a way to survive and thrive.

Apparently nothing does as much damage to New York City sewage and water lines as tree roots. If there isn't enough rainfall getting to their roots through that two-foot square in the sidewalk, they start looking for an alternate supply. What could be better than a pipe full of fresh water running just below street level? City workers aren't so thrilled with the vandalism, but I can't help but cheer for the trees. An army of plucky, streetwise sycamores, maples, and elms taking on the rigid confines of their city life, and quite literally breaking free.

A Stinky Lesson

The fairest thing in nature, a flower, still has its roots in earth and manure.

— D. H. LAWRENCE

Every spring when I was a kid my father would rent a tilling machine and push it through the muddy ground on a plot at the back of our yard. I was fascinated and would spend long days hanging around and helping plant corn, beans, tomatoes, and other vegetables. But my favorite thing were the flowers, and of those, the zinnias.

Hearty, easy to grow, and improbably bright and varied in color, they still remind me of those happy days in the sunshine spent weeding, watering, and pruning. My least favorite part of the whole process, I have to say, was fertilizing. My father was delighted when a friend offered to haul over a load of manure from the local horse stables. He urged me to help as he spread the stuff all around the newly planted garden, but I sniffed at the endeavor and skipped off to other pastimes.

When the zinnias came up a few weeks later, I noticed something strange. Half of them were growing fast and hearty, and while the others were coming along, they didn't look as healthy or as bright. My father smiled as I peered at them, and I realized then that he'd arranged a bit of a lesson for me by not fertilizing that patch. And I haven't forgotten it since.

Sticking it out through an unpleasant (or smelly!) task now can pay handsome dividends later.

53

Being an Unnatural

His talent was as natural as the pattern that was made by the dust on a butterfly's wings. At one time he understood it no more than the butterfly did and he did not know when it was brushed or marred.

— ERNEST HEMINGWAY

You've heard people say, "Oh, she's a natural artist" (or athlete, or student). Whether it's said with admiration or jealousy, there's a kind of finality to that statement. We're meant to understand that nature should get most of the credit for all this person's current and future accomplishments. Don't forget, too, that we should harshly judge our own natural dearth of talent in a wide array of pursuits. Uh-oh, I smell trouble.

Sure, it can be great fun to do something well right away, easily exceeding the standards or the expectations of those around you. Only when that first elation wears off do you realize you may have lost an opportunity to grow, or to learn something new. While you were feeling very self-satisfied and proud, someone else without your natural ability was working her tush off and learning a whole lot in the process.

The only antidote is to become an "unnatural." That is, to seek the thrill of the challenge and the reward of failure in everything you do. The joy of living is in striving, in doing, and in overcoming obstacles.

Broaden your expertise (and your confidence) by developing some skills that don't come naturally.

Everything's Coming Up Dirt

The pursuit of truth and beauty is a sphere of activity in which we are permitted to remain children all our lives.

— ALBERT EINSTEIN

Imagine the gifts that the courage to be honest might bring into your life.

A children's storyteller shared this fable with me.

The emperor of China is coming to the end of his life, and he has no heir. He loves flowers, so he decides that he will pass out seeds to all the children in the land, and the one who grows the most beautiful flower shall be the next ruler of China.

One little boy plants his seed in a beautiful pot in rich soil, gives it just the right amount of water, just the right sunlight, and even sings a little song to the seed every day. But nothing grows. Weeks pass, and still nothing grows. The day to return to the palace approaches, and the boy is ashamed of his empty pot, but his father tells him that if he has done his best to grow a flower he must go before the emperor without shame.

The other children in line at the palace have beautiful flowers, and they tease the boy for daring to bring an empty pot. But each pretty flower gets a gruff *Humph* from the emperor. Finally the boy approaches and holds the pot up, closing his eyes in terror. The emperor lets out a huge, roaring laugh and says, "I don't know where the rest of you got your flowers, for the seeds I gave you were boiled. Only this boy had the courage to come before me with an empty pot, and only this boy is fit to be the next emperor of China."

Do Your Worst

Diligence is a good thing, but taking things easy is much more restful.

— MARK TWAIN

Make some time to slack off and break free from the stress of trying to be perfect.

I've been reading about perfectionists; I tend to count myself as one. As a child I would break down sobbing if I couldn't do a new task or solve a problem easily and quickly. I have always judged myself harshly and felt that I could do better—sometimes pushing myself to the point of exhaustion. But it should come as no surprise that perfectionism, though widely praised in our culture, can lead to more serious mental trouble, including eating disorders, obsessive-compulsive disorder, and even suicidal tendencies.

We always tell ourselves to "do our best," no matter the situation, but what about when doing our best at every single thing is wearing us out and stretching us thin? One remedy for perfectionism is to consciously do your *worst*. It doesn't have to be your worst at everything, but pick something and do a bit worse than you'd like to do, and see what happens. Force yourself to take it easy, cheat on your diet, leave the crossword unfinished, and skip scrubbing the bathroom tile. Then step back and see if the world crumbles around you. Most likely nothing terrible will happen (unless you're an airline pilot or a brain surgeon—you folks keep on being perfect, please) and you'll gain the added bonus of a little perspective on your life.

The Beauty of Being Busy

My candle burns at both ends;
It will not last the night;
But ah, my foes, and oh my friends—
It gives a lovely light!

> —EDNA ST. VINCENT MILLAY

One of my mother-in-law's best friends has taken in foster children over the years. Despite excelling at a full-time job with lots of overtime hours and being a single woman over fifty, she has fallen in love with and eventually adopted three babies who came into her life this way. Talk about exhaustion: working all day and coming home to care for kids who have a host of physical and developmental difficulties. Her love for them has multiplied by the day, making manifest their dreams and helping them grow into strong, gifted, healthy children and teens. What a reward.

It seems to me that our job in this life is to give love, and I admire tremendously those among us who burn the candle of their love brightly at both ends in the service of others. Yes, it may wear them down, and the workload may feel like too much to bear at times. But life is short, and what better way to spend it than to savor the results of your hard work and love? Imagine if all of us gave as much as we could, and we all got to feel that exquisite exhaustion.

Instead of letting your busy schedule wear you out, remember the love that guided your decision to give this much of your time and energy, and let that love energize and inspire you.

An Unwelcome Guest

As welcome as a skunk at a garden party.

— PROVERB

Don't forget that one unpleasantness may be canceling out a worse one.

In college I lived in an apartment at the end of a row of houses bordered by a wooded area. One spring when the snow had pretty much melted but it was still cold at night, we had a visitor. Every night for about a week I would come home to find a skunk in the front yard, just steps from the door. Not having any other way to get in the house and not wanting to get sprayed, I would wait at a safe distance and watch him. He seemed to be rummaging around in the grass, and I wondered if someone had spilled something there or if there was loose garbage out.

It was an annoyance to have to wait in the cold—once for nearly an hour before he ambled off—and I didn't have the first clue about what to do about this unpleasant situation. It wasn't until a week or so later, when the ground started to warm up a bit, that I realized the service this skunk had been providing. I looked more closely at the holes he'd been rummaging around in and saw that a colony of wasps had been nesting in the ground in our front yard for the winter. There were only a few wasps coming and going, and I gave complete credit to that skunk, who had probably slurped up quite a few of the pesky creatures.

Everyday Beauty

Beauty is not caused. It is.

— EMILY DICKINSON

How can you bring beauty to a difficult or boring task today?

My mother lives in a city neighborhood bordered on one side by a steep hill. There are houses built all the way up the hill, and winding streets that curve around them. On several of the streets that run into the hill, the sidewalk turns into steps. The hill is so steep it's like someone took a normal city block and tipped it, and steps were the only way to go. You can imagine what it feels like to trek up a city block's worth of steps, straight up. It can be a great way to stay in shape or a major pain in the behind, especially if you need groceries and you don't drive.

Maybe that's why the people in the neighborhood decided to start painting murals and creating mosaics on the front faces of the steps. They are beautiful—swirling waves filled with fish and other sea creatures that lead up to mountains, sky, and a crescent moon. You look at them as you walk and all sort of things come to mind—stories, memories, thoughts of the artisans who planned and drew and sat on those steps to make what you're seeing. What could be a functional, boring walk brightens up with the artists' touch, and you're at the top in no time.

Pretty Trashy

Small minds are concerned with the extraordinary, great minds with the ordinary.

—Blaise Pascal

When I was moving into my first apartment my mother told me, "Get a nice trash can. It's worth it."

"What?" I thought. "Why have something pretty and well designed to toss your egg shells and used dental floss in? Who cares?" So, like the rebellious child I have occasionally been, I didn't take her advice. I got something ugly and plastic with a lid that looked destined to crack (which it did a month into its stay). If you work at home even part of the time, you spend a lot of time walking to the trash can and then more time opening it up and closing it. Well, every time I went to throw something away in that grungy, poorly designed can, my mother's sage advice rang in my ears. *Humph.* Right again.

At the core of her good advice was an appreciation for everyday tasks and the time and energy it takes to do them. She doesn't believe in a well-designed, good-looking trash can for its own sake, but because she's a smart mama she knows that looking at something annoying and ugly all day is going to bring you down, while making an investment in the beauty of functional things makes our hearts lighter and our lives better.

Next time you want to splurge, consider gussying up some ordinary thing you use every day.

And a Child Shall Teach Us

Children are born optimists and we slowly educate them out of their heresy.

—Louise Imogen Guiney

Enlightened writers and thinkers are always praising the genius of children. It seems that the older we get the less likely we are to keep our eyes open, expect the best, or use our imaginations. Yet I think if we adults were magically thrust back into a child's life we might be overwhelmed. My kid grew almost an inch every month of his life until he turned two. Imagine the stress of growing at that extraordinary rate while trying to keep up with people more than twice your size. Think of the frustration of a toddler trying to communicate a desire without knowing the right words or even having the muscle coordination to articulate clearly. I'm not sure I could handle it.

Reeducate yourself to see life's challenges like a child: positive, proactive, and resilient.

Kids manage to maintain their resilient happiness even as they work through difficult challenges. They don't gripe about the obstacles they're facing at preschool or obsess about physical shortcomings. They just get busy exploring and discovering their world. Beyond that, children seem to have an innate belief that things are going to work out no matter what. Even when they're afraid or tentative, they manage to stay open and optimistic. We could all do well to rediscover our inner child.

Creative Cubicle

Don't be a cynic and disconsolate preacher. Don't bewail and moan. Omit the negative propositions. Challenge us with incessant affirmatives. Don't waste yourself in rejection, or bark against the bad, but chant the beauty of the good.

—RALPH WALDO EMERSON

Find a way to add a splash of creative color to your day.

I recently saw a "worst cubicle" contest in a magazine. Workers sent in photos of their miserable working spaces—laptop perched on a cardboard box in a windowless cube shared with two other people, an unheated tractor trailer converted into an office.

The contest made me remember a particularly dismal temp job I had once. The office where I was assigned was made up of rows and rows of narrow cubicles with no natural light, and even the people who worked there seemed to be taking on a grayish pallor. Then, on my way to the coffee room, I saw a flash of bright color. One employee had decorated her small space top to bottom with pictures cut out of magazines—it was a mosaic of tropical locales, bright red dresses, flowers, and trees. In another setting I might have thought it tacky, but the effect in the space was brilliant—a beacon of creative color in the sea of conformity.

Comfort in the Eye
of the Storm

Think of all the beauty still left around you and be happy.

— A N N E   F R A N K

My best friend's house was flooded last summer, and she told me the story of coming home with her daughter and husband to find the place in total chaos. Books and papers were strewn everywhere and there were brown mud stains 2 feet high on everything. She took it all in, a bit in shock. It might seem strange, but the most vivid memory she has of that whole day is a huge vase of peonies on the fireplace mantel. It was one of the only things in the house left untouched, and the pale pink flowers were at their peak, as big as heads of lettuce.

In the midst of devastation, keep something lovely and calm in your mind and heart.

The sight comforted and calmed her as she started the task of cleaning up the mess and finding out what was gone and what could be saved. I don't know if I would have been calm enough to even notice those flowers, let alone allow that image to permeate my recollection of such a tragedy.

Flowers will continue to bloom no matter what—and there will always be beauty in the world. Maybe that's why we give and receive flowers on the occasion of an illness, tragedy, or loss. They calm our nerves and serve as a reminder of the cycle of all things dying and being reborn.

A Life in the Clouds

Be faithful to that which exists nowhere but in yourself—
and thus make yourself indispensable.

—ANDRE GIDE

What is your essence? Do you know? In hard times, reconnect with the beauty at your core.

I had a friend who had a miserable time as a teenager. Several family tragedies, major problems in school, and a cross-country move had left her stripped bare—anxious, guarded, and fragile. As a senior class project, several of us decided to take photographic portraits of everyone in the class, and it took a long time to gain her trust, but she finally agreed to let me take her picture. We went to her favorite place, a hilltop outside of town, and she lay down in the grass with her eyes closed. She had just checked her face in a compact mirror, and she absent-mindedly laid it right at her throat.

Most of the class pictures came out fine, and they were nothing too special, but the ones with the mirror still stay with me. You didn't notice the mirror right away, so at first glance it seemed strange to see the edge of a cloud reflected at her neck. It was as if the girl was made up of sky, walking around on the ground with clothes on and her feet in some heavy shoes, but ready to float away at any moment to return to her life in the clouds.

I caught up with her years later and found she was thriving—happily working as an artist and spending plenty of time with her head in the clouds, dreaming up new projects.

Vertical Thinking

We spend most of our time and energy in a kind of horizontal thinking. We move along the surface of things . . . but there are times when we stop. We sit sill. We lose ourselves in a pile of leaves or its memory. We listen and breezes from a whole other world begin to whisper.

— JAMES CARROLL

Our lives today move faster than ever before. Convenience is a necessity, multitasking is a given, and relaxation is a luxury. No wonder we burn out and sit in front of the TV whenever we get a chance. In the midst of it all, it's hard to remember that while we may feel too worn out to do anything more than tune out, what we really need is time to tune in.

When we devote so much of our time and energy to horizontal thinking and the quick evaluation of the surface of things, we starve our minds of the vertical thinking we need. We all do better when we get a chance to delve deep into our thoughts, memories, and desires.

Through vertical thinking—and living—we start to see the beauty beyond the everyday grind. When we tune in to our subconscious, we feel more and more comfortable swimming under the surface reality that limits and demoralizes us. We draw strength and insight as we sound new depths. We can return to the surface any time, bearing the gifts of hidden beauty and truth.

Next time you catch yourself paddling along the surface of your life, go ahead and plunge in.

Face into the Wind

You cannot find peace by avoiding life.

— VIRGINIA WOOLF

As we get older we may think that the best way to stay healthy and active is to stick to what we know. Trying to get out and learn new things can confuse us, frustrate us, or sap our energy. Not so.

I just heard an expert talking about how our brains get older and stop functioning as we'd like them to. Like a muscle, the tissue in our brains deteriorates over time, but the brain is such an amazing organ that it can work around and make up for losses and regain function. Think of a patient recovering from a stroke relearning basic skills.

Find greater peace by facing life's struggles and challenges head-on.

We spend most of our childhood exploring and learning new tasks, and as we get older we spend more and more time practicing skills we already know well. The repetition of familiar tasks and routines contributes to deterioration of the brain—if you don't use it, you lose it.

Those people who can find ways to continually engage in tasks they care about and that challenge them have better brain health. Not only do they maintain better memory skills and overall brain function, but they also feel better. Those synapses firing away contribute to our sense of self, of feeling energized and motivated to face life.

Three
Door Closes, Window Opens

Door Closes, Window Opens

When I lived in Italy during my junior year of college, I rented a room for a couple of months on the top floor of a tall apartment building. From my window I could see a huge chunk of sky and the old part of the city in the distance. It was summer, and every evening at around five o'clock a thunderstorm emerged from a clear sky, and an hour later it had passed completely. You can imagine the wind it took to carry those heavy clouds in and back out in such a hurry. Because it was so warm, I left the window open as well as the little door out to a patio balcony. As the storm approached, the door would often slam shut, and with the force of the pressure change inside the room, the window would fly open. I always forgot to prop the door, and so I'd jump out of my seat with the noise.

The image has stayed with me. When I don't get a job I was trying for, when all the stoplights turn red on my way to an important appointment, when the universe seems to be screaming "No" and slamming the door on my every desire, I tune in and look for the "Yes" window. Sometimes it's tiny, but it's always there. The pressure of "No" always builds up and finds a "Yes" outlet somewhere, just like a thunderstorm blowing fresh air through a stuffy room.

Sometimes that "Yes" isn't so obvious. Sometimes we don't even recognize it as a "Yes" until days, months, maybe years, later. Sometimes we need to go looking for it, and, yet, when we look too hard, we can't find it. Often it means reframing the way we look at "Yes" and "No," and changing our lives in the process.

A Rite of Passage

When it is dark enough, you can see the stars.
— C H A R L E S A U S T I N B E A R D

Sometimes it takes the door hitting you on the way out to open your mind to the possibilities beyond those four walls.

"You're fired!" Two words most of us dread. You're not up to the standard at the job, or you aren't pulling your weight, or it's a difference of opinion or just a plain old clash of egos. In the moment it happens, what could be worse? Your livelihood, your pride, your confidence have all suffered a body blow.

I've only been fired once, and I won't go into too many gory details, but let's say that in the weeks leading up to the event my focus wasn't on the tasks in the job description. After it happened, I started to walk the city streets, no idea where I was going. It was fun for an afternoon, and then I had a panic attack. What if I never found another job? What if everybody in the whole world (including all potential future employers) somehow knew? What if I just had that "fired" look now? I called my favorite aunt and began to sob.

"Oh, sweetie, are you kidding? Getting fired is a rite of passage—you're not a real adult till you've been canned. Take it from me, I'm a real adult ten times over, give or take."

I hung up the phone, took a deep breath, and suddenly my mind was racing. Maybe it was the first real adult brainstorm of my life, and it got me back in school, doing what I love, and infinitely happier for it. Thanks, cranky old boss—I owe ya one.

Stalking the Unknown "Yes"

For my part I know nothing with any certainty, but the sight of the stars makes me dream.

— VINCENT VAN GOGH

I recently saw a television show featuring Deepak Chopra, the spiritual teacher and lecturer, who was talking about waking up every morning thrilled about life and hoping for as many surprises as possible. He said he tries to embrace the unknown, because he believes that all of life really is unknown; we walk around pretending it is known when it is really in some essential way unknowable and unpredictable.

I've thought about that for weeks now—it comes into my head nearly every day. I spend more time than I'd like to admit wishing for the known, hoping that I will encounter situations, people, and problems that are familiar to me and that I feel confident I can handle. Any confidence I beg or borrow doesn't come from inner strength; it's based purely on the illusion that if I know what's coming I know how to deal with it.

Imagine the true confidence that must come from being on a hunt each day for the unknown. Imagine finding a way to feel secure in the face of a world that is changing before your eyes, in which every moment bursts forth completely different than any that has come before. Of course, this *is* the world we live in, and instead of trying to predict outcomes and generate results, maybe it's time to go on a hunt for the unknown.

When you wake up tomorrow morning, say out loud, "Universe, I'd like as many surprises as you can muster today, okay?"

Investment Portfolio

Allow yourself to want things, no matter the risk of
disappointment. Desire is never the mistake.

— PAULA McLAIN

*Time to throw out the
balance sheet on your
relationships and the
pursuit of your dreams,
and make an investment
in your heart's desire.*

I have a playwright friend who was lamenting the other day
that he'd put too much work into a recent project. Beyond the
time he'd spent on it, he'd poured so much of himself into
the play, and he was worried that nothing would come of his
hard work, that nobody would respond to the piece, and that
it would get stalled and never have a life beyond readings and
workshops. He felt he'd put too much work into it for the
amount of return.

We all want to feel that what we care about and work
hard at is important, valued, and cherished by other people.
Sometimes, for whatever reason, we don't get the payback we
feel would make it all worthwhile. That makes us feel silly,
like we care too much. When you're doing what you love to
do and you're learning and growing, there's no such thing as
caring too much.

In the world of business and finance, return on investment is the measure of success, but we sell ourselves short
when we try to apply that yardstick to our emotional, artistic, or moral endeavors. You can't put too much love into rais-
ing a child, for instance, but no amount of love ensures that
the kid won't get sick or won't grow up to be an ungrateful
cur. And countless enlightened souls have taught us that you
can't have too much faith or be too selfless.

Lemons and Lemonade

The Constitution only gives people the right to pursue happiness. You have to catch it yourself.

— Benjamin Franklin

Next time someone hands you sour lemons, suck it up and pour on the sweet stuff.

The same aunt who soothed me when I was fired has a great saying: "You can't make lemonade without a little sugar." Kind of a cross between "When life hands you lemons, make lemonade" and "You catch more flies with honey." Her point is that you can't fight sour with sour.

If someone's rude or nasty to me, my first instinct might be to throw that energy right back at them. I know it probably won't help the situation very much, but it's hard to resist the instant gratification of getting back at someone. Of course it often creates a much bigger problem in the long run, and later I regret not having been able to look at the situation more calmly.

I remember being in the car with my aunt once when she was pulled over for speeding. Boy, you could have scraped the honey off that cop and sweetened your tea for a year. The poor guy never knew what hit him, and my aunt drove away with a warning and a smile. "See, darlin?" she said. "You can't make lemonade without a little sugar."

Serendipity

Serendipity. Look for something, find something else, and realize that what you've found is more suited to your needs than what you thought you were looking for.

— LAWRENCE BLOCK

Serendipity trumps brooding intellect any day. It's easy to plod along with your nose to the ground looking for the solution to a difficult problem, blind to the happy accidents floating around in the air around you.

Your grandmother is driving you crazy, calling every day telling you she hears a mouse in the wall. Finally in desperation you rescue a big tomcat from the local animal shelter and bring him over. The daily calls stop and you get some peace, and when almost a week goes by and you call to make sure she's okay, she tells you, "Oh, honey—you should get a kitty—if you're calling me for no reason you might be lonely." You realize the cat's an even better companion than he is a mouser.

Or: you teach your teenage daughter to sew a patch on her ripped jeans. It's a quick fix and saves some cash. Next thing you know she's got a side business at school designing cool patches.

Or: Your contractor tells you the wall in your bathroom is rotten and needs to come down. You pay him up front and when he starts the demolition he finds a stash of Prohibition-era $20 bills tucked away in there.

Things don't always turn out as we expect, and sometimes that's a blessing in disguise.

Lucky Old Nag

The only sure thing about luck is that it will change

— BRET HARTE

Keep your eyes open for hidden opportunities, sly gifts, and unforeseen blessings.

There's an old story about a farmer who is given a horse. The man dotes on his eldest son, and he offers the horse to the young man as a present. On his first ride, the horse bucks the kid and he lands hard, breaking his arm. The man thinks the horse is bad luck and decides the gift was a bad omen and he should get rid of the horse as soon as possible.

The next day, Army recruiters come to the farm to collect any able-bodied males to take off to war. Of course, the son cannot go because of his broken arm and is spared. The father rejoices.

The story reminds me to trust in the unknown and unknowable and to hold off with my curses and bad omens until the whole story of an apparent misfortune plays itself out. Sometimes luck touches us in a roundabout way.

Intentional Mistakes

If the fool would persist in his folly he would become wise.
— WILLIAM BLAKE

Next time you make a mistake, look for the secret upside (and the tiny footprints).

Mistakes are the fairy godmothers of silver linings. Call it serendipity or whatever you like, sometimes nothing brightens our day better than a good "Whoops!" or two. A wrong turn that leads to the perfect parking spot, noticing an error while balancing the checkbook that leaves you with more money than you thought you had.

Then there are intentional mistakes—ever make one of these? This is a blunder that comes courtesy of your subconscious. Like when you're so tired you set the alarm but forget to turn it on, and this forces you to get some much-needed rest. Or misdialing the phone and finding out the person you called by accident had been trying to reach you all morning with an urgent message. In relationships, an error in judgment might lead to a huge fight, but in the end you learn something about the other person that you never knew, and it deepens your connection in the long run. The fairies may be at work here, even if you don't believe in them. Pulling you this way and that, calling the shots so that you land right smack where you need to be to meet your destiny.

Go Granny Go!

Trouble is only opportunity in work clothes
— HENRY J. KAISER

The other day I picked up my grandma Millie to take her out to dinner. We didn't have a reservation at the place I was hoping to go, but I dropped her off in front so she wouldn't have to walk if I couldn't find a parking spot right in front. Two blocks down I found a great spot, and as I started to pull into it a young woman stepped into it with her hands on her hips, shaking her head at me. She pointed down the block to where her boyfriend was backing up five cars away to take the spot.

I fumed, stifling the urge to scream at her, and drove on. Did she have any idea my poor granny was waiting, none too thrilled to be chatting up a maitre'd? As I carried on out loud about the injustices in this world I made a couple of right turns and came upon a place to park directly in front of the restaurant. Only trouble was there was an old lady standing right in the middle of it. But as soon as she recognized me, she waved me right in. On top of that, my granny had already sweet-talked the guy into the best table in the house.

Don't trouble yourself with lost opportunities, just make a few more turns and you'll probably come upon something better. Especially if you've got a feisty ally or two on your side.

Endurance Training

I have not failed. I've just found 10,000 ways that don't work.

— Thomas Alva Edison

My friend Carol found her second child more exuberant—and more exhausting—than her first. His energy level was so high that he had quite a lot of trouble winding down for bed. Not uncommon, not worrisome; it just made for some long nights, some early mornings, and a very tired mama.

So she came up with a plan to wear him out, to use up any energy he had left in the day by taking a long walk after dinner. It seemed to help at first, and he fell asleep and stayed asleep longer for a week or so. After that, the effects started wearing off, so she kept making the walks longer. Hearing about their treks, her mother called one evening to check in. From her cell phone as they walked, Carol moaned, "This isn't working—I'm just building his endurance."

Mothers have incredible endurance—maybe more than they thought possible before children came into their lives. They can function on almost no sleep, even remaining lucid enough to accurately measure cough syrup and make up perfect bottles at 2 a.m. Getting things done faster and more efficiently, multitasking, motivating themselves and others, all the while staying cheerful enough to banter with a three-year-old. Carol was really building her own endurance for a host of tasks that would serve her in all aspects of her life.

What menial or strenuous tasks in your life are making you faster, stronger, and wiser?

Giving Back

What we have done for ourselves alone dies with us; what we have done for others and the world remains and is immortal.

—ALBERT PIKE

What gifts will you leave for those you love to cherish and remember you by?

On the train I ride there's a poster that shows a picture of Jerry Orbach, the Broadway and television star who passed away in December 2004. The text of the poster reads, "Jerry Orbach gave his heart and soul to acting, and the gift of sight to two New Yorkers." It seems that he was always proud of his sharp eyesight and decided several years before his death to make an organ donation. I've always had trouble checking that box on the back of my driver's license for organ donation. Like most of us, I'm terrified of my own mortality and would rather not dwell on the particulars of what happens to my body when I'm gone. It seems disrespectful to my body parts to take them out and shuffle them around into other people. But reading about how much Jerry's family admires him and his decision, I'm realizing that this kind of gift is the ultimate respect for the body we're given—to recycle any working parts back into the stream of life.

While it's clearly a life-changing gift for the receiver, it also offers those left behind a memory that lives on in a very concrete way, a final act of love that transcends death. This can be true in every mourning process; however we pass from this life, we leave behind gifts in this world for now and later that provide comfort and solace for a long while.

New Growth

Life's challenges are not supposed to paralyze you, they're supposed to help you discover who you are.

— BERNICE JOHNSON REAGON

Every year there are stories on the news about wildfires burning through vast areas, threatening or destroying homes and businesses. These can be devastating, lasting for days or weeks and causing millions of dollars of damage. For years the policy on forest fires was to eradicate every one immediately, but that changed in the 1960s. Someone realized that no new Giant Sequoias—the largest trees in the world—were growing because wildfires are an integral part of the life cycle of these trees. Their seeds are locked in huge pinecones, often very high off the ground; small fires heat the cones, which dry and release their seeds. The fires also clear the soil below of competing plants and enrich it with nutrients, providing the perfect springboard for a baby giant to start growing.

Ease up on your protective impulses and live a little more deeply.

The lesson for me in this is to remember that while we take precautions to protect ourselves from extreme danger, we may sometimes be eliminating the possibility for new growth. If we tie ourselves to our job in the hope we will never go without, we may find that new technology outpaces our understanding and we are left behind. If we fear being rejected by those we care about most, we may close our hearts to new and deeper levels of intimacy. It's only by accepting the risk of some painful trials that we get to experience the joy of new growth.

Making Room

Let the dream go. Are there not other dreams
In vastness of clouds hid from thy sight
That yet shall gild with beautiful gold gleams,
And shoot the shadows through and through with light?
What matters one lost vision of the night?
Let the dream go! . . .

— ELLA WHEELER WILCOX

One school of thought is that we should hold on to our possessions, relationships, jobs, and, yes, dreams—at almost any cost. Make it work. Work at making it work. And, yes, sometimes—maybe often times—that's a really good philosophy to live by. But maybe not always.

Letting go of a thing—say a lost cell phone or wallet—isn't easy. And I'm pretty sure losing them wasn't your dream for the day when you walked out the door this morning. When we lose a phone or a wallet, we have a choice. We can lament the loss, or we can pull up our socks, do what we need to do and go on. I like to consider it practice for making room for something else in my life.

Sometimes making room is all about attitude. I know a woman in her sixties who "gave up" her dream of being a poet. That's what she said about herself. What she really gave up was her idea of being a famous, published poet—read, revered, and making a living doing it. Not only that, but she "gave it up" for a wonderful career helping writers find their own voices, editing books, and, yes, writing some poems.

Do you have any old dreams that need to be released to make room for some new ones?

91

Stirring Things Up

Life loves to be taken by the lapel and told: "I'm with you kid. Let's go."

— MAYA ANGELOU

Break free from your everyday drudgery by going on an unplanned adventure.

When my husband was a child his mother would sometimes pick him up from school on a Friday afternoon with the car loaded full of camping supplies for the weekend. "Where to?" she would ask him. He'd pick a direction and off they would go on an unplanned, spontaneous adventure.

They had some of their best vacations that way—leaving the journey up to chance, staying open to whatever neat thing caught their fancy. Often times they ended up sleeping in the car, and still having a blast. As he got older and looked back, he realized that sometimes those trips were his mother's ingenious way to get them out of a rut. Maybe he'd had a bad week at school, or maybe his mom was struggling to find a job, but they could always make their own decisions about where to go and have a great time for a couple of days.

My husband's mother taught him that when times are tough you can always take matters into your own hands and try to enjoy the ride. Regardless of where they ended up on their weekend adventures, they always came back renewed and refreshed, their routine jostled out of its everyday monotony. Sometimes life even responded to the shake-up of routine with a pleasant surprise: a job interview, a helping hand, or a chance at something new.

The Success of Failure

I am pretty fearless, and you know why? Because I don't handle fear very well; I'm not a good terrified person.

— STEVIE NICKS

"If I were a good typist, I'd never have been a CEO."
"If I hadn't broken my leg that summer, I never would've learned to draw and paint."
"If I had been an obedient daughter, I never would have learned to fly helicopters."

What you can't do well may give you the gift of what you can.

There are countless stories of people whose planned direction in life went off course only to reveal a deeper, more natural, and maybe unexpected path to success.

Though she'd done well in school and was extremely smart, my friend flunked out of med school. Even though it was what she thought she wanted to do and it was most definitely the future her parents had in mind, she found her heart wasn't in it. She took a huge leap of faith and applied to acting schools to get a master's degree and got into one of the best in the country. Now a successful and happy actor, while she was failing in med school she never imagined that she was laying the groundwork for a success that would be true to her own passions.

Every failure gives us information about ourselves, and each stumbling block can be a signpost to try harder and jump an obstacle, or a big fat arrow pointing in the opposite direction. Either way, it'll most likely lead you right to where you need to be.

Reverse Psychology

If you wish to forget anything on the spot, make a note that this thing is to be remembered.

— EDGAR ALLAN POE

Outsmart yourself with a little backward, upside-down, or reverse thinking.

When I used to babysit as a teenager, my mom taught me a few tricks for dealing with toddlers, my favorite of which was reverse psychology. "Don't you dare eat those peas!" I would admonish, and the kids would crack up as they shoveled in the veggies, thinking they were getting away with something sneaky.

It seems that even adults are prone to the effects of this stuff. I know I am. My husband asks me to clean the tub, and I forget to pick up that tile scrubbing stuff we need for a week straight. Try to remember when to check the oil in the car and it flies out of my head again and again. Try to forget that song from *Sesame Street* and it sticks to me like glue.

Maybe I should try a little experiment on myself. Every time I feel like reverse psychology is getting the better of me, I'm going to get it back. I'll be spontaneous while on deadline, I'll make lists and throw them away, I'll get people gifts for their not-birthday, or just because. That'll show me.

Seriously though, maybe it's time to forgive our lapses in memory or judgment and go with whatever windows our psyche opens up, and not ponder over any closed doors. Maybe all is just as it should be, either way.

Four

Weathering Storms, Celebrating Rainbows

Weathering Storms, Celebrating Rainbows

Suffering is a given in this life. Even if we escape the list of awful things that could possibly happen, there are still the troubles of growing up, growing old, and dying. And regardless of how well we prepare, each new storm sees us battening hatches and praying for the best. To get through bad weather and difficult times, we need strong hearts, close friends, and inspiring stories. I've heard people say that the release from pain feels better than never being in any pain in the first place. Difficult times, illness, injury, and loss all bring us the lesson of gratitude. We come out the other side renewed: stronger, wiser, and more able to experience the joy all around us.

It's true—what could be better than the moments after a storm? Just the other day I was driving under some of the most beautiful cloud formations I've ever seen. It had been raining for two days straight with no letup, and finally the sun broke through and the bank of clouds rolled on to the east. You appreciate the sun so much more after a few days without it: the plants are happier, the air smells fresh, and a weight is lifted from the world. So as you gaze at all the silver linings on the receding clouds, remember how lucky you are and celebrate!

The Rocky Bottom

You gain strength, courage, and confidence by every experience by which you really stop to look fear in the face. You
are able to say to yourself, "I lived through this horror. I
can take the next thing that comes along."

— ELEANOR ROOSEVELT

Every end is a beginning,
and sometimes the best
way to reach the highest
heights is to start over
from the lowest low.

I can't say I've ever hit what I would call rock bottom. Even
though I've had my share of disappointments and losses, I've
always felt very lucky never to have felt that last, sinking feeling. Or maybe I've never let myself get there.

Why is it that some people seem crushed by extreme circumstances and some are able to bounce back better than
before? Is hitting rock bottom really a gift? Just as a person in
hysterics may need a slap across the face to be able to focus,
a person in trouble may need to crash land on rock-hard
ground before he can begin to evaluate his situation and
understand his options.

It can be a relief to get to that place you thought you
could never recover from and realize with a deep breath, "I'm
still alive. *Now what?*" Even if you never come to see the positive side of whatever dragged you so low (a destructive fire,
a death, a divorce), the chance to start over is a gift.

Near Death

Miracles are instantaneous, they cannot be summoned, but come of themselves, usually at unlikely moments and to those who least expect them.

— KATHERINE ANNE PORTER

It happened several years ago, but I just heard a first-person account of Czech model Petra Nemcova, a survivor of the tsunami in Indonesia who lost her boyfriend in the disaster and was rescued after spending eight hours clinging to a tree. She described a first wave that brought the debris that crushed her pelvis before it released her, and then a second wave that pulled her under. She said she struggled, gulping down the black water, but at some point she stopped, very calmly realizing that this might be her time to go and putting all of her trust and faith into the universe. Strangely enough, she related, it was the most peaceful moment of her life, and shortly afterward the wave released her again and she saw the beautiful blue sky.

Release your expectations, calm your soul, and you may be pleasantly surprised.

If we struggle against our fate and thrash around in opposition to the universe, we may miss the miracle that's waiting for a quiet moment of release to make its grand entrance.

Cow Pies

Wealth is but dung, useful only when spread.

— CHINESE PROVERB

Invite your inner child out in the open to savor some messy, smelly, or squishy fun, and spread the wealth around.

Ever stepped in dog doo? What could be worse? You shuffle through a grassy patch trying to get it off, but you can't possibly. So you end up working your way through a whole roll of paper towels. And then you think it's gone but you can still smell it. So while you valiantly try to keep down your lunch you do some vigorous scraping and scrubbing and then have to throw away a perfectly good dish brush. Or a perfectly good pair of shoes. Or both. Surely, there is no silver lining here.

Then I remember my father. A farm boy from Wisconsin, he often extolled the virtues of a fresh cow pie. If you don't know to what I am referring, let me just say that despite its rich color it doesn't have an ounce of chocolate in it. He could've cared less about the fertilizing properties of the stuff, or the fact that some people in far-off lands use it to build homes and heat them. No, he loved it when it was so fresh it was still warm, fresh enough that he could jump right in and squish it between his toes. You can imagine his mother was thrilled. But her annoyance was probably just icing on the cake for a mischievous, thrill-seeking farm kid.

Older, Wiser, and With Better Hair

The age of a woman doesn't mean a thing. The best tunes are played on the oldest fiddles.

—RALPH WALDO EMERSON

Most women I know don't look forward to aging. I myself had a minor freak-out the other day after glancing in a mirror hanging under a bright florescent bulb. My skin had gained a whole new texture, and far too much of it is migrating south, leaving some nice big wrinkles as it goes. Remember, I admonished myself, wrinkles come from smiling and laughing just as much as worrying, so if you're going to get them you might as well have a good time doing it. Then I slapped on some moisturizer for good measure.

Most women also dread their hair going gray. My mother didn't feel all that strongly about it, but her hairdresser had convinced her that she'd better not go down that road gracefully. So she submitted to a yellowish blonde that looked nothing like her youthful hair. She hated it, and she eventually gave up and started growing it out.

On a trip to visit me she came along to my hairdresser, who's a good friend. "My god!" my friend ranted. "Why would anyone ever try to cover up this color—it's gorgeous." She cut off the old, dyed color, and my mother looked amazing. The streaks of gray, white, and black were a beautiful complement to my mom's skin tone. In the wash of feminine vanity, she never realized how lucky she was to be going gray.

Is your vanity getting in the way of a newer, fresher, more authentic you?

Cosmic Harmony

The ground we walk on, the plants and creatures, the clouds above constantly dissolving into new formations—each gift of nature possessing its own radiant energy, bound together by cosmic harmony.

—RUTH BERNHARD

Bring the perspective of a larger, cosmic harmony to bear on your troubled moments.

Sometimes everything comes together. It might happen walking through the woods, or taking a bath, or driving in the zone on a lovely road. The beauty of your surroundings suddenly clicks, and all is well with the world. I feel that those moments sneak up on me, and I savor them while they last.

There is a mountain near where I grew up, a place where you can go and see long stretches of woods and river. It's a place I will always feel welcome, and where that feeling of serenity seems easily available. Being up high, surrounded by nature—I can forget for a while the pressures of life in the man-made world.

I've found that I can access this place without physically going there. In a moment of strife or stress I can find a quiet place and sit down, close my eyes, and mentally travel the road to the top of that peak. I imagine walking to the very edge of a cliff and looking out, taking in the meeting of earth and sky. Through this meditation I calm down and celebrate the beauty of all things connected in the natural world, and from that mental vista, my problems shrink back to their real, manageable size.

A Place to Call Home

The bird a nest, the spider a web, man friendship.

— WILLIAM BLAKE

Friendships are the homes we build for ourselves—the people we love and who love us, our soul's nurture, the people with whom we tend our dreams and shape our realities. I recently read a study about elderly widows. Those who do not have close friends pass soon after their spouses, but those who enjoy a close female friendship are much better equipped to heal and carry on, and live much longer, more fulfilled lives. Friends are literally lifesavers in the toughest storms.

Take some time today to tell a friend how you feel, or do something that will make her day.

I sometimes catch myself taking friendships for granted, forgetting how essential they are to me, in good times and bad. When a friendship is strong and solid, this is easy to do. It may feel like you don't have to do anything to make it work or to enrich it for the future. Just as with any other relationship, friendship needs regular care and tending. It needs special time without spouses and kids, it needs silly emails and late-night rambling phone calls.

With regular care and maintenance in the easy times, you'll find your friendships weatherproof and strong when storms come blowing through.

The Upside of Adversity

He that wrestles with us strengthens our nerves, and sharpens out skill. Our antagonist is our helper.

— EDMUND BURKE

You couldn't train to be a boxer, a fencer, or a great tennis player without an opponent. Sure, you could drill, jump rope, practice your moves, but without somebody to try it all out on, you can't develop beyond a certain point. You need an oppositional force coming at you fast and furious to train your body and mind into shape.

When the going gets tough, the tough are growing.

Top athletes push themselves and each other. What about when it seems like your circumstances are your adversary, throwing punches you're not sure you can handle? The most successful people in all realms use adversity to their advantage: to broaden their experience, hone their intelligence, and challenge their imagination. So the next time you feel a bit sorry for yourself because the going is getting tough, remember that anything that pushes you helps you. In fact, when you feel things might be too hard to handle, you are probably at the very brink of a breakthrough to becoming stronger and wiser.

Long Journey

Because the road is rough and long,
Shall we despise the skylark's song?

— ANNE BRONTË

Keep your eyes and ears open to the beauty around you and stay positive—if you can, no journey will be too long or arduous.

The pessimists I know tend to think within the confines of their own experience, while the optimists I know are able to look outside of themselves no matter what they are going through and see the beauty around them. It's cause and effect —the more we dwell on our own rough journey, the less we can see what is positive around us, and the worse we feel. On the other hand, the more we notice the wonderful sights and sounds along the rough road, the less attention we pay to our heavy load and blistered feet.

Every difficulty will come to an end, and we always have a choice of how we're going come out on the other side. Is it worth it to moan and complain, only to have the task of licking your wounds when it's all over? Isn't it better to stay as positive as you can, so that when you look back on hard times you have an equal measure of good memories to celebrate and treasure?

Helping and Healing

To ease another's heartache is to forget one's own.

—ABRAHAM LINCOLN

I met a woman on an airplane once who was on the first leg of a three-part flight to Africa to work with a humanitarian organization that was providing fresh water to remote villages. She looked like she was in her early sixties—and she told me she hadn't done much traveling abroad, but after her husband died recently she decided she wanted to go and offer her services.

Shifting your outlook from yourself to others can have a huge positive effect—not only for you, but also for those around you who need help and solace.

I can't imagine what it must be like to lose your life partner, to be left with a house full of memories and faced with a new life without that constant. I would probably be inclined to sit at home for a while, maybe reach out and connect with family and friends to ease the grief, but I don't know that I would have the courage to do what this woman was doing. In the face of fear and loss, she was throwing herself headlong into new experiences, with the needs of others at the center of her journey.

I don't know the rest of her story, but I'm hoping that the challenges and rewards of her trip went a long way toward easing her heartache. I know it inspired me to think of helping others in my worst moments.

Calm After the Storm

I've learned that no matter what happens, or how bad it seems today, life does go on, and it will be better tomorrow.

— MAYA ANGELOU

Don't forget that every drama winds down, every explosion tapers off, and sometimes the rainbow after the storm is even better than the sunshine that came before the clouds.

Scientists this year observed a geomagnetic storm traveling 400 miles through the sky in a minute and releasing as much energy as a 5.5 earthquake. And you know what the effect was on Earth? The Northern Lights. Every day we are hit with the leftover energy exploding out of the sun, and here on Earth it amounts to the wonderful feeling of sitting in a warm sunny room on a spring morning.

Sometimes big, powerful events scare us. Perhaps rightly so—I don't think I'd want to spend much time in the eye of a geomagnetic storm. As energy dissipates and spreads, the benefits become clearer. Just so with dramatic events in our lives. The initial shock overwhelms us and floods our senses. Afterward, as things run their course, we can feel the gentler, more positive effects.

It's important to remember when we get hit with a particularly difficult time that "this too shall pass." Every storm has to run its course. No wind can blow forever, and rain can only come down in sheets for so long before the clouds empty themselves out.

Waking Up

Wake at dawn with a winged heart and give thanks for
another day of loving.

— KAHLIL GIBRAN

I had a teacher once who told us that the best way to start
your morning was to do what he did. Every morning, he
woke with the sun, drank a glass of water, and strode down
to the lake near his house. Then he walked into the lake up to
his neck, in slow motion. Then turned around and walked
back out, very slowly. He's totally nuts, I remember thinking.

One day on vacation near a lake, I tried it. I woke up earlier than I ever do, as the sun was rising. I put on my bathing
suit and walked down to the lake. It was late summer and
already getting chilly at night, so there was a cold mist over
the water. I stepped in. *No way,* I thought, *I can't do this.* But I
decided to tough it out.

It was a simple, active meditation—just walking, breath-
ing, getting used to the cold, and trusting I was going to be
okay. *I can't do this,* I kept thinking. *I can't do this!* my mind
screamed as I got into deeper water. But I kept doing it, and
I found that I could.

It was so cold and miserable going in, I was surprised to
find that as I came out my blood was pumping warm through
my whole body, my brain was alive and awake, and I was
ecstatically happy. I still remember it as one of the best days
of my life.

*Plan a day to get up
with the sun and do
something that will
wake up your body,
mind, and heart.*

Thankful in the Here and Now

We don't know what we've got until it's gone.

— PROVERB

A week or so ago I hurt my neck trying to lift my kid up for a shoulder ride. All I did was hoist him up, just like I've done a hundred times before, and—Bam!—the spasms shuddered through my neck and down my spine, and it was everything I could do to land him safely in my husband's arms before I dropped him. Later, as I lay motionless on a heating pad for hours in front of the TV, I started to think about how lucky I am.

Aside from some pretty silly accidents and injuries, I've never been seriously hurt. And if a simple shoulder tweak could lay me out like this, I can hardly imagine what it's like to survive a car accident or something even worse.

I got the lesson loud and clear, again, about appreciating the incredible mobility I have while I have it, not waiting to bemoan it when it's gone. Being sore after a tough workout is a huge gift—it means my muscles are working and growing stronger. Gaining five pounds over the holidays might be mildly frustrating, but I am hugely grateful to have good food to share and a wonderful rag-tag family to enjoy it with.

Make a list of things you're thankful for, so you can quit whining and better appreciate what you've got, no matter how long you have it.

Fairytale Endings

If you can see the magic in a fairy tale, you can face the future.

— D A N I E L L E S T E E L

The deepest darkness gives way to a bright happy ending, and we all cheer, so pick up a good book and savor all the gory details.

For my niece's sixth birthday I got her a complete set of *Grimm's Fairy Tales*. My sister pulled me aside later and said, "Hey, thanks for the book but I think I'm going to have to put it away for a few years—have you read those things lately?" This is my sister who to this day will fast-forward through the forest fire in Bambi and the witch scene in Snow White. A week later I got a call. "I'm going to kill you," my sister said. "She loves them. It's all we can read before bed now."

"Does she have nightmares?" I asked.

"No, but I do. Thanks a lot," she replied, and hung up.

Wolves eating grandmothers, evil stepsisters, witches trying to cook little children in an oven. I understand her point. Part of why those stories compel us so much is their cruelty, the characters' struggles, and the grand drama of it all. I get why my niece loves them, because I do too.

It's fun to read a story with danger and struggle and get afraid. We're human beings; we live for this stuff. A fairytale ending has to be earned. The more cackling, sneering, and crying on the way, the better.

Thank-You Letters

Gratitude is a vaccine, an antitoxin, and an antiseptic.

— JOHN HENRY JOWETT

A friend's mother recently won her battle with breast cancer. Many people who get sick have a hard enough time finding the energy to focus on themselves and their own recovery, but somehow my friend's mom felt that she needed to actively reach out to others throughout her illness, not just to get support to cure herself, but to give whatever she could, no matter how much time she had left.

Gain strength and perspective by writing down what you are grateful for and sending it along.

One day she started writing thank-you letters. She asked her daughter to bring her a box of note cards, and she spent the week writing them out. Thanking people for flowers or letters of encouragement, then thanking others for their friendship. Even writing to politicians working for causes she admired and to artists whose work she loved. Everyone who visited her brought her stationery, and every time anyone left, they carried a stack of notes for the mailbox. My friend told me her mother eventually started to write letters that would never be delivered—to deceased aunts, famous novelists from centuries past, even mythological figures. There was a letter, my friend told me, to cancer itself. A thank-you letter, can you imagine?

I can't help but think that her recovery had something to do with that constant outpouring of gratitude and the positive energy she put into the world and received in return.

Acknowledgments

Thanks to everyone at Conari Press for their support and understanding.

Special thanks to Bob and Louise Rosen, Darlene Rodriguez, Mattie and Bill Tirey, Susie and Jean Pral, Denise Reber, Jan Johnson, Larisa Johnson, Jessica Taube, Sam Soule, Crystal Skillman, Denis Butkus, Daniel Reitz, Julie Kline, and Stephen Willems.

Most special thanks of all to Daniel and Bailey Talbott.

To Our Readers

Conari Press, an imprint of Red Wheel/Weiser, publishes books on topics ranging from spirituality, personal growth, and relationships to women's issues, parenting, and social issues. Our mission is to publish quality books that will make a difference in people's lives—how we feel about ourselves and how we relate to one another. We value integrity, compassion, and receptivity, both in the books we publish and in the way we do business.

Our readers are our most important resource, and we value your input, suggestions, and ideas about what you would like to see published. Please feel free to contact us, to request our latest book catalog, or to be added to our mailing list.

Conari Press
An imprint of Red Wheel/Weiser, LLC
500 Third Street, Suite 230
San Francisco, CA 94107
www.redwheelweiser.com